Dearest Caydan,
Food is a gift - learn & share in it with love & care for it. Find the extraordinary in the ordinary - it's there - I promise!!
Love Your friend,
Dr. DeSouza-Kenney

Nutritious and Delicious

A fruitful conversation for kids

LEANNE R DE SOUZA-KENNEY, PHD

Illustrations by Stefanie St. Denis

Nutritious and Delicious
Copyright © 2017 Leanne R De Souza-Kenney, PhD

No part of this publication may be reproduced, distributed, or transmitted in any form or by any means, including photocopying, recording, or other electronic or mechanical methods, without the prior written permission of the author, except in the case of brief quotations embodied in critical reviews and certain other non-commercial uses permitted by copyright law.

Tellwell Talent
www.tellwell.ca

ISBN
978-1-77302-593-3 (Hardcover)
978-1-77302-594-0 (Paperback)

To my Mom and Dad, Martha and Stephen and to my
Sister, Darlene, for making sure everything was possible.

To my Husband, David and to my Children,
Oliver, Sebastian and Augustin,
for making me believe in the impossible.

Let's talk about food!
What are some of your favourite foods to eat?

My favourite foods are

Nu-tri-tious

Let's say it together, nutritious!

Can you guess what nutritious means?

Nutritious foods are good for us because they have nutrients that make us *strong* and *healthy*.

Nutritious foods help us *grow*.

Nutritious foods are also

De-li-cious

Delicious is a word that means so yummy, so tasty, so wonderful to eat!

What are some of your favourite
nutritious and delicious foods?

Did you know that we should try to enjoy foods that are nutritious *and* delicious at each of our meals?

Can you name some of the nutritious *and* delicious foods in this picture?

Let's look at this picture of 2 meals.

Can you choose which meal is more nutritious and delicious?

Now try choosing which dessert is more nutritious and delicious.

We can make our favourite meals, snacks and desserts with ingredients that take them from delicious to nutritious *and* delicious!

Let's think of some ingredients that we can use to make this birthday cake more nutritious and delicious.

When you go to the grocery store, there are many foods to choose from that are nutritious and delicious.

You can explore and try some new foods that you might enjoy.

We can learn about healthy, tasty food by helping out in the kitchen and cooking together.

When we eat with our family and friends it is a special time to have conversations and to learn about each other, while enjoying the nutritious and delicious foods that we made together.

Now let's put everything we have learned
into a rhyme to help us remember!

Nutritious and delicious foods are fun to eat!
At breakfast, lunch or dinner time and in between as treats.

My favourite snacks and desserts are so de-li-cious!
Even they can be made to be nu-tri-tious!

We can eat together and learn about each other.
Eating is a special time to share with one another.

So learn to cook and try new things and surely you will see,
Healthy food is tasty food and good for you and me!

The End...

and
The Beginning
of your

Nutritious

and

Delicious

journey!

HOW TO GET THE MOST OUT OF THIS BOOK

NOTES TO PARENTS AND TEACHERS

Nutritious and Delicious: A Fruitful Conversation for Kids is a short guide for kids and parents, guardians and teachers, that is intended to be read together with a fun, interactive approach. The conversational format of this book is deliberate in order to stimulate ideas and opportunities for learning, lead by readers and their individual, ever-changing experiences about what they know and continue to learn about nutrition and making food choices on a primary level.

The learning is inherent in the conversations that children or groups of children may have while reading or being read to. Returning to the book from time to time should evoke new knowledge and ideas based on individual development and perspectives (hopefully inspired by lessons learned by reading this book in the first place).

In addition to the learning that no-doubt will take place with little ones spearheading the conversations using their boundless creativity, enthusiasm (and predilections about their favourite foods), below are a few ideas to help enrich their experience with this book and their potential to reap life-long lessons from its simple messages.

1. Word recognition! The first instance of the words 'nutritious' and 'delicious' are spelled out in large coloured font with the letters separated in order to emphasize meaning and to stimulate word recognition. These words are intentionally repeated throughout the book.

2. As our little Beans learn about the definitions of nutritious and delicious (greatly simplified in this book), here is a fun learning activity that can be applied to reinforce the lesson.

   This creative project requires kids' safety scissors, a non-toxic glue stick, recyclable paper plates and some flyers from local food stores. Instruct children to cut out their favourite nutritious and delicious foods and paste their choices on the plate in order to 'build a meal' and a healthy dessert. Children can explain their choices, which can be reflected on in relation to the lessons learned in the book. A follow-up activity would be to help them plan a recipe that they can prepare with the help of an adult.

3. An adaptation of the activity in #2, would be to simply flip through your local food flyers, pointing out items and having children name the foods that are nutritious and delicious and those that are less nutritious (perhaps even suggesting their alternative, more nutritious renderings).

4. As the back of this book describes, this interactive book began with our family navigating early childhood and by extension, early parenthood. The grocery store may not seem like an obvious choice as a field trip or bonding expedition for the family, yet there are a plethora of experiences and opportunities for learning that can enrich the curious, developing, inquisitive minds of our children. These are the opportunities to inject our culture, family values and life lessons that extend beyond the classroom and the routines prescribed by our daily agendas.

We play a game in the grocery store that you might enjoy and tailor to your family needs. The premise of the game is to have children point out (dare I suggest, put into your buggy) nutritious and delicious foods. Inevitably, some super tasty foods that are less nutritious will suit the fancy of your little one. Here is the opportunity to have a conversation about alternative options about how we might treat ourselves, but augment the treat with some other more nutritious item (for example page 17 shows a dessert plate reflecting a reasonable portion size and a more nutritious and well-rounded option). If time permits, you might even make the food item from scratch, taking the opportunity for your little one to choose nutritious ingredients for your homemade concoction (as demonstrated on pages 18-21).

 Leanne De Souza-Kenney, Ph.D., received her doctorate in Medical Science, specializing in diabetes prevention, from the University of Toronto. She has a Master's in Nutritional Science from U of T and 15 years of teaching experience. Leanne grew up in Toronto, Ontario where her parents worked while managing a Bed & Breakfast with the B&B Homes of Toronto. Migrating to Canada from Goa, India and witnessing her parents' resilience and commitment to providing an enriched life, inculcated values toward family bonds, exotic foods, faith, culture and community. Dr. De Souza-Kenney is actively involved in teaching and research at U of T and she lives with her three children and husband in the greater Toronto area.

◉ leanne_desouzakenney

My Learning

Notes, Questions, Ideas and More

CPSIA information can be obtained
at www.ICGtesting.com
Printed in the USA
LVOW06s1543031017
550829LV00001B/1/P